45010     371. 425 FN

Books are to be returned on or before
the last date below.

LIBREX—

45010

Rebecca Faulkner | **How to get ahead in**

# Finance

# www.raintreepublishers.co.uk

Visit our website to find out more information about **Raintree** books.

To order:

 Phone 44 (0) 1865 888113

 Send a fax to 44 (0) 1865 314091

 Visit the Raintree bookshop at **www.raintreepublishers.co.uk** to browse our catalogue and order online.

First published in Great Britain by Raintree, Halley Court, Jordan Hill, Oxford OX2 8EJ, part of Harcourt Education.
Raintree is a registered trademark of Harcourt Education Ltd.

Editorial: Melanie Waldron and Lucy Beevor
Design: David Poole and Calcium
Illustrations: Geoff Ward
Picture Research: Melissa Allison and Fiona Orbell
Production: Huseyin Sami

Originated by Chroma Graphics
Printed and bound in China by South China Printing Company

10 digit ISBN 1 406 20448 X
13 digit ISBN 978 1 406 20448 3

11 10 09 08 07
10 9 8 7 6 5 4 3 2 1

**British Library Cataloguing in Publication Data**
Faulkner, Rebecca
Finance. – (How to get ahead in)
658'.002341
A full catalogue record for this book is available from the British Library.

**Acknowledgements**
The publishers would like to thank the following for permission to reproduce photographs: Alamy pp. 35 (ACE STOCK LIMITED), 33 (BananaStock), 10 (Bob Johns/ expresspictures.co.uk), 14 (Frank Herholdt), 7 (Photofusion Picture Library), 37 (Rob Bartee), 22 (Stock Connection Distribution), 49 (Stock image/Pixland), 23 (The Hoberman Collection); Corbis pp. 45 (Gerard Steiner), 13 (Larry Williams), 17 (Left Lane Productions), 6 (Matthias Kulka), 20 (Royalty-Free), 4 (zefa/ A. Inden), 21 (zefa/G. Baden), 26 (zefa/Larry Williams), 32 (P. Windbladh); Getty Images pp. 39 (DigitalVision), 25 (Gulfimages), 9 (ImageBank), 18, 36, 16, 34, 46 (Photodisc), 43 (Stone), 11 (Taxi); Harcourt Education pp. 30, 47 (Tudor Photography); Manchester Business School p. 51; reportdigital.co.uk p. 29 (Paul Box).

Cover photograph of young businessman reproduced with permission of Getty Images/Digital Vision.

The publishers would like to thank Stephen Yeats for his assistance in the preparation of this book.

# Contents

Words appearing in the text in bold, **like this**, are explained in the glossary.

What do you imagine when you think of a career in the finance industry? Do you see yourself as a city banker working long hours on multi-million pound deals, earning enough money in bonuses to buy a sports car every year? Or do you see yourself as the **bank clerk**, working 9 to 5 in your local bank? These are just two of hundreds of different types of careers in the finance industry. Finding all the information to help you decide if this is the career for you can be difficult. That is where this book comes in. It will give you an introduction to what the finance industry is, what sorts of jobs it offers, and will help you decide if you would like to work in this industry.

**above:** *If being outside in the great outdoors is what you crave, a career in finance may not be for you.*

It is very important to find the career that suits you so that you will be happy in your job. To find the right career needs a lot of careful thought and planning. This book aims to help you make the right decision.

# Get ahead!

This book cannot tell you everything about the finance industry – it can only give you an introduction. To find out about the organizations that interest you, you will need to visit their websites, or write to them. You can also get more advice from your careers advisor at school. They will be able to help you choose the right career.

When you think of the finance industry, what is the first thing that springs to mind? Banks? Banking is big business and employs a large number of people in a huge variety of jobs. In the last 30 years, however, banking has changed dramatically. New technology, such as the introduction of cash machines, telephone banking, and the Internet, has reduced the numbers of staff needed in traditional jobs.

# Get ahead!

Make a list of as many financial products and services as you can think of. For each product or service, write down where you would be able to buy it. You will need to think of other places, in addition to banks.

On the plus side, the new technology has created new jobs, for example, in IT and **call centres**. There are still plenty of opportunities for careers, but competition for jobs is likely to be fierce.

The finance industry as a whole is growing. It employs over 1.25 million people in the United Kingdom. The ever increasing need for financial services, such as savings, **pensions**, insurance, and **mortgages**, means that the industry will continue to grow in order to meet these needs. This development provides excellent opportunities for careers, both in traditional customer-facing roles and in increasingly sophisticated IT systems. Although jobs are available throughout the UK, many are based in London and the south-east of England. These are the areas closest to the financial centre of the country, which is in London and is often called the City.

# CHANGING TIMES

Thirty years ago there were no cash machines in the UK and no such thing as a **credit card**.

# Chapter 1

# What is the finance industry?

Before you read any further, let's think about what finance actually means. Finance means anything concerned with money. You will have already made financial decisions in your life such as how to spend, or save, your pocket money. You may already have a **bank account**. If you decide to go to university after you finish school, you will have to take out a **student loan** to pay your **university fees**, and may find it difficult to avoid having an **overdraft**. When you start earning money, you may want to take out a mortgage to help you buy your first home. All of these activities, the bank accounts for paying in your **cheques**, the student loans and the mortgage, are everyday examples of financial services.

## The finance industry

The finance industry involves a wide range of activities to do with personal and **commercial** finance. There is much more to it than the bank clerk who works in your local high street bank. The range of careers in the finance industry is immense. As well as high street banks, employers include accountancy firms, investment banks, and insurance companies.

**below:** *Finance is the business of money.*

The different sectors of the finance industry are described below. As you read through, think about whether one or more sectors appeal to you more than the others do.

### Retail banking

When you think of working in banking, do you imagine

**above:** *There are many different retail banks; some are a lot larger than others.*

sitting at a counter all day, taking in and paying out cash? This is certainly one component of the retail banking industry, but there is much more to it than that.

A retail bank is the kind of bank you will find on your local high street, which is why they are given the alternative name "high street bank". You may have visited your local retail bank many times, to use the cash machine or to pay in a cheque. Retail banking is big business. It operates at many levels, and is not just a place where you have your bank account.

Many retail banks also offer telephone banking and Internet banking. In order for these to operate 24 hours a day, they are supported by call centres, which provide an additional source of jobs in the finance industry.

## Get ahead!

Visit three different banks in your local area. Find out what accounts and other services they offer to someone your age.

## PROTECTING YOUR INTERESTS

The whole finance industry is **regulated** by an organization called the Financial Services Authority (FSA). This organization is very important, as it makes sure that all finance industries stick to certain rules.

Today, banking is very much customer-focused. This means it aims to provide top quality services to customers, whether they are individuals, small businesses, or large businesses, and whatever their financial needs. Banks compete for their customers, so they offer many different types of services, from mortgages to car insurance to credit cards. If you work in a retail bank, you could be working in a department that deals with personal accounts or you could be working for a department that deals only with business accounts. In all cases, it is your responsibility to make sure that the service is delivered.

### Investment banking

Investment banks offer a wide range of services and often have offices in many countries. They arrange deals between companies such as **mergers**, **acquisitions**, and **take-overs**. They trade **stocks** and **shares** on the **stock market**. Trading means buying and selling. Just as a fruit and vegetable trader sells produce at your local farmers' market, so a financial trader buys and sells stocks and shares on a financial market. Examples of jobs in investment banks include financial analysts, stockbrokers, and traders.

**Get ahead!**

Search on the Internet for the names of some investment banks. Write to them and ask them what services they offer.

### Investment management

Investment management or fund management companies look after money, for example, from pension schemes for businesses and governments. They advise businesses on how to manage their money. They also **invest** businesses' money in companies listed on the stock exchange that have shares to sell.

### Accountancy

Accountancy involves creating and analysing all the financial information of a business. All companies need to provide accounts, so there are many career opportunities in this area. Some accountants check a company's financial accounts to make sure they are reporting them correctly. Other accountants will advise companies on how to plan their finances, manage their money, and draw up their accounts.

## Insurance

Insurance is one of the UK's most important **service industries**, employing approximately 250,000 people. Insurance provides protection for companies and individuals for loss or damage to belongings, illness, or death. Insurance is a huge industry. Ask your parents what types of insurance they have – they will possibly have house insurance, car insurance, health insurance, and travel insurance. They are also likely to have life insurance, which will provide **compensation** to the family in the event of death.

The insurance industry offers a wide diversity of career opportunities from **underwriting**, **brokerage**, and claims through to investment analysis and financial advice.

In this chapter you have looked at the main areas of the finance industry. You will now go on to look at specific jobs that you could do within this diverse industry.

**right:** *Working in travel insurance means you could be dealing with all sorts of holiday accidents!*

# Chapter 2

# What types of jobs are available in finance?

The finance industry offers a huge range of jobs, from accountant to stockbroker, to call centre staff to city trader. Opportunities for work exist throughout the UK, although most jobs are found in London. There are jobs at all levels – management, professional, skilled, and semi-skilled. Every job is different and every person has different expectations about what they want to achieve in their career.

Read through the following jobs and try to decide if any of them appeal to you. If they don't, this does not mean a career in finance is not for you. This is just a small selection of the vast array of possible jobs that exist within the industry.

### Bank clerk

As a bank clerk, you are the public face of a retail bank, so you are the person who will deal with customers when they come into your bank. You will look after customers' bank accounts, paying in and withdrawing money using computerized systems, and answering queries. You will also sell the bank's products and services to customers and may arrange loans. Some clerks are based in call centres, where you would deal with customer queries over the phone.

**left:** *As a bank clerk you will be responsible for dealing with the bank's valuable customers.*

right: *Fund managers must analyse the changing values of a company's stocks and shares to decide whether or not to invest money in it.*

## Fund manager

Fund managers are very powerful people. They work for investment, or fund, management companies, and invest money from universities, councils, or companies. As a fund manager you need to do lots of your own research to find out where to invest your clients' money. Fund managers often deal with huge amounts of money and you need to be able to predict how a company's investments are likely to perform, otherwise you may end up losing millions of pounds for your client.

## Branch bank manager

A branch bank manger is responsible for running one branch of a retail bank. In this job you will be responsible for organizing the staff, attending meetings, and preparing reports for head office. You will also need to motivate your staff in order to meet targets for selling the bank's products such as mortgages and loans.

## Stockbroker

Stockbrokers work for investment banks. They are the people who buy and sell stocks and shares on financial markets. Stockbrokers advise their clients, or fund managers, on which stocks and shares they should buy and sell. The fund manager may then ask the stockbroker, or "broker", to buy or sell the shares, and the broker will take a **commission**.

### Accounting technician

An accounting technician works alongside an accountant and may work for an accountancy firm, a bank, or a large company. You may advise a company on financial matters such as how to keep records of their accounts. You will work with qualified accountants creating accounts for companies, listing all their **income** and **expenditure**. This will involve collecting lots of financial data and writing reports. You could be working for all types of businesses, from small local companies up to huge international organizations.

### Financial advisor

A financial advisor might work independently or for a retail bank, and will advise customers on a wide range of financial issues such as mortgages, insurance, pensions, and investments. As a financial advisor you therefore need a broad knowledge of all these services, and of who offers the best deals.

### Insurance broker

An insurance broker is similar to a financial advisor, but only provides advice on insurance. You would advise people on what different insurance policies offer and try to find the best policy for the customer. The job involves a lot of research, looking at the different policies from different insurance providers, and then selling these policies to customers.

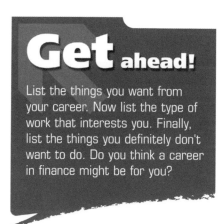

# Get ahead!

List the things you want from your career. Now list the type of work that interests you. Finally, list the things you definitely don't want to do. Do you think a career in finance might be for you?

In this chapter you have looked at just a few of the many and varied jobs in the finance industry. In the next chapter you will move on to look at what you can expect your working environment to be like, should you choose a career in the finance industry.

# Chapter 3

# What will the working environment be like?

Do you prefer to work in a large, open-plan office, or do you need your own quiet space to concentrate? Do you like to know what you have to do each day, or do you like surprises? In this chapter you will begin to get an idea of the working environment you can expect for jobs in finance.

### What do you want?

You need to think about you career choice carefully. Different people want different things from their careers. You may want:

◎ a challenge
◎ a lot of money
◎ the opportunity to meet lots of new people
◎ a chance to be part of a team
◎ to work 9.00 a.m. to 5.00 p.m. rather than long hours
◎ a chance to develop your skills.

Most people try to work in the finance industry "to earn a lot of money". While this may happen for some people, the reality is that you will start at the bottom of the scale and have to work long hours if you want to reach the top at an investment bank.

**left:** *Do you like the idea of working in a large, open-plan office with lots of different people?*

## Working conditions

Working conditions vary in the finance industry but it is likely that you will be working in an office, spending a lot of time in front of a computer screen, sitting at a desk, or meeting clients. You will also be expected to dress smartly. You could be working for an organization of any size, from a huge open-plan office in a retail bank to a small financial advisor's office where you may be working with just one or two others. Some of your work may involve travelling to visit clients. This may be in the UK or abroad, and may involve overnight stops.

**above:** *International travel may be part of your job. If you are lucky, you will get to fly business class!*

Simon works as a stockbroker.

*I work normal office hours, from 9.00 a.m. to 5.00 p.m. I go into work, sit at my computer and advise, and then receive instructions from my clients. I spend a lot of time on the phone and I act on behalf of my clients. When I'm not on the phone I am either in meetings with clients or writing reports.*

*My job is probably not as exciting as you imagine it to be. Since I work on North American markets I get two trips to North America per year. This part of the job sounds exciting, but I usually have a very hectic schedule of meetings with companies and conferences to go to. As a result, I end up seeing very little of the country. I do like meeting new people, though.*

Some careers in finance can be highly pressurized, with long, irregular hours, especially in investment banks. Other jobs, such as financial advisors, offer greater flexibility, with home working, part-time, and self-employment opportunities. Telephone banking operates 24 hours a day, so shift work is common, and you could end up working through the night!

# CASE STUDY

Rachel works as a telephone operator at a bank call centre.

*I don't just work bank opening hours. I usually work shifts, either from 10.00 a.m. to 6.00 p.m. or from 1.00 p.m. to 9.00 p.m. I often have to work at weekends as well, and sometimes all through the night as we operate 24 hours a day. If I work a weekend I will get 2 days off during the week, so it's not as bad as it sounds.*

## A typical working day?

In general, for most jobs in the finance industry, you will normally work office hours, from 9.00 a.m. to 5.00 p.m., Monday to Friday. You will, however, be expected to work longer hours at busy times, especially at the end of the **financial year**, in March.

In investment banking you may be expected to work much longer hours. You may need to start at 6.00 a.m. and finish at midnight in order to trade on international markets working in different **time zones**. Much of your day will be spent in a busy, tense, and pressurized environment.

The best people to tell you about a typical working day in the finance industry are those who work in it. Below are some examples.

## CASE STUDY

Justin works as a clerk for a retail bank.

*I work normal office hours, but also have to work every fourth Saturday. The bank is looking at increasing its opening hours, so I might even have to work some Sundays in the near future.*

*I work face to face with the public for most of the day, usually on the foreign exchange desk. As well as attending to customers in the bank, I also deal with telephone enquiries, and make up the currency orders. At the end of the day I order money for the following day and make sure that the stock levels are OK for the next day.*

## CASE STUDY

Frieda works in the Japanese Department of an investment management company.

*The nature of my job means there is always something to learn and read up on, so there's never a typical day. My day starts early. We have a team meeting at 8.00 a.m. The rest of the day is spent researching Japanese companies, to find out if they would be good companies to invest money in. I may also have meetings with clients or companies.*

*I usually work long hours and my job can be very pressurized. It is a fast-paced, multitasking environment to work in. I work to tight deadlines, so it is important to be able to work well under pressure and manage your time.*

**above:** *You may find yourself working against the clock, long into the night.*

## CASE STUDY

Lena is a manager of a retail bank.

*I work long hours, from 7.30 a.m. to 7.00 p.m., but on the plus side I never have to work weekends. I have a lot of control over what I do each day, so I can make my job as varied as I like – no two days are the same. A typical day will involve me meeting with customers to discuss mortgages (this may involve some travelling). I also have to do a lot of paperwork, for example, arranging meetings, processing mortgage applications, and attracting new customers. I keep staff up to date by giving them daily briefings on sales targets and what I expect them to do that day.*

# How much will I get paid?

For some people, this is the most important question when deciding on a career. As you are thinking about working with money, this may well have been your first question!

Salaries and **benefits** for financial jobs are among the best available in any industry. Having said that, rates of pay vary a lot depending on:

◎ your specific job
◎ where you work
◎ the size of the company
◎ your experience
◎ your qualifications.

If you join a retail bank straight from school, for example, as call centre staff or as a bank clerk, you can expect to start on a **salary** of around £10,000 to £15,000 per year. If you join a bank as a university graduate you will earn more, in the region of £16,000 to £24,000 per year. In addition to a salary, most financial institutions will also provide benefits such as pension schemes, **subsidized** mortgages, and often subsidized insurance.

**left:** *Be warned: not everyone working in the finance industry can expect to earn huge bonuses.*

Successful accountants can expect to earn high salaries, but a school leaver just starting out can expect to earn between £10,000 and £17,000 per year, depending on your work and your responsibilities. As a new graduate, you will earn between £12,000 and £22,000. Once you are qualified, your salary will rise to between £27,000 and £40,000.

Traders, stockbrokers, and fund managers can earn upwards of £100,000 a year plus bonuses. These bonuses can be huge, sometimes more than the salary, so for some the dream of buying a sports car with your bonus can become a reality.

### Finance's millionaires

There are only a few exceptional individuals who earn the huge salaries and even bigger bonuses you may have seen reported on television or in films. For these few, their combined salaries and bonuses are likely to be in the region of £1 million a year.

## CASE STUDY

Sasha works as a recruitment manager at a retail bank.

*My working conditions are excellent. I started 2 years ago as a university graduate, and now earn £28,000. I work in a team and we all get along very well. Some people in this industry earn huge amounts of money, but not when they start out at 18 years old. In addition to my salary, I have an excellent pension scheme and life insurance cover.*

# Chapter 4

# Am I the right person for the job?

You will know by now that there are many different types of jobs in finance, attracting many different types of people. This means it is difficult to pinpoint one set of skills that you will need for whatever job you are applying for. You will find there are opportunities for many different types of people.

In this chapter, you will look at the main personal qualities and skills that might be useful for jobs in the finance industry.

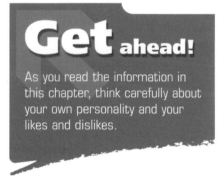

## Get ahead!

As you read the information in this chapter, think carefully about your own personality and your likes and dislikes.

### People skills

The ability to get on well with people is important in most jobs, and the finance industry is no exception. If you are dealing with customers on a face to face basis in a bank, for example, you will need to be able to relate to many different types of people. Banks are competing for their customers, so unless you can provide excellent customer service, the customer will simply go elsewhere.

**left:** *You will need to remain calm and courteous even with customers who may be upset or angry.*

Richard works as a bank clerk.

*In my job the customer is very important. I have to be able to talk to customers in a friendly way and get on with them. I have to be patient, because even though there may be a long queue of people to get through, I still have to be polite and chatty with the customer I am dealing with. If you don't like meeting people then you would have a problem working in this job. I meet with customers on a daily basis, so you have to enjoy meeting new people all the time, otherwise you would have a very miserable time at work.*

## Communication skills

You need to have strong communication skills, both written and spoken, and be a good listener. At school you will have plenty of opportunities in your English lessons to develop these skills, and it is very important that you do.

As a fund manager, you will need to listen to your clients' needs and preferences, write reports on companies you think would be suitable for investment, and be able to make presentations to small or large groups of people. When you are asked to do some research for homework, this can be a good way to practise these skills.

**below:** *You will need excellent communication skills to meet and deal with lots of different people.*

Meena is a partner in a stockbroker firm.

*My company is very small, which means I get to do a broad range of jobs. I deal with clients, usually over the phone, but sometimes in the office. You have to be a good listener. I think this is one of the most important skills. If you don't listen to what your clients want, they will not want to deal with you. My job is stressful, but I enjoy it. My company recruits staff for their personality not just their qualifications. The ideal person would be responsible, a good communicator, and able to use his or her **initiative**.*

### Numeracy and computer skills

Information technology (IT) is important in the financial industry, so you need to have good IT skills. You will also need to be good with numbers for a lot of the jobs in the finance industry. If you work hard and do well in your Maths and IT lessons, you could be on track for a finance career. It is especially important to learn how to use Microsoft Excel, as many jobs in the finance industry require you to keep track of figures in this way. Whether you are a bank clerk, accountant, or stockbroker, you will be dealing with figures, so you will need to be comfortable with this.

**below:** *Many finance jobs will require you to have a good head for numbers.*

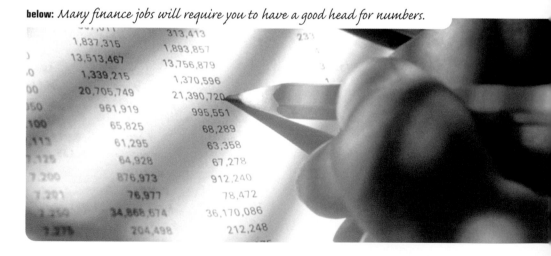

### Analytical and research skills

You will need good analytical skills for jobs in investment banks and fund management companies, as you will often have to analyse data and make decisions, sometimes very quickly. You will also have to be able to research and understand complicated financial information, using your skills and knowledge to analyse it, and think of solutions to problems.

## Ambition, drive, and commitment

In addition to the qualities mentioned above, to work in an investment bank or fund management company you need ambition. This type of work attracts high fliers and there is strong competition for jobs, so you will have to fight hard to get one. The rewards can be huge, but so can the responsibility. You will be dealing with huge amounts of other people's money, so you will have to be able to cope with this while appearing professional at all times.

Abid works for an investment management company.

*My company's clients are large organizations. They trust us to manage their money for them, so we have to be very professional. We need to make them feel confident that we are investing their money wisely otherwise they will take their money elsewhere.*

*It helps if you are ambitious and determined to get on. This will help you cope with the long hours and responsibility that goes with the job. This is a fast-paced business and I am often dealing with huge amounts of money, so you need to be self-confident, decisive, and competitive to be successful.*

**below:** *You will need a lot of drive and energy to work as a trader – every day you will have to act quickly and think even more quickly!*

In accountancy, investment banking, and fund management you will need to work towards professional exams. This will require determination and commitment, and it is essential that you still have a strong desire to continue studying even after university. You need to be able to cope with studying for exams in your own time, so these types of jobs are not for you if you are not willing to work hard.

## CASE STUDY

Debbie works as an accountant for a car manufacturer.

*I am currently working towards becoming a chartered accountant. The company pays for the course and gives me time off work to sit the exams, but I have to do all the studying in my own time. All accountants have to train hard and pass a lot of exams, but you get a great sense of achievement at each stage.*

### Working long hours

For many senior jobs in the financial industry, you need to be able to cope with long working hours. There may also be travel involved, for example, you may need to get a 6.00 a.m. flight to Frankfurt for a meeting and then be back in your office in London for a meeting at 5.00 p.m. the same day.

### Working under pressure

As a trader, one thing you need to be able to cope with is working under pressure. There will be constant pressure for you to perform well and get results. If you fail, you are likely to lose your job, so you also need to be able to cope with the uncertainty of how long your job will last.

### Taking risks

Both traders and stockbrokers need to be risk takers, and it helps if you are confident, determined, competitive, and outgoing. You need to be able to cope with making quick decisions involving huge amounts of money. You will also need to be able to absorb and analyse a lot of detailed information on which to base your decisions.

*right: Many large companies will have offices abroad, so if you work in their financial department you may get the chance to travel.*

# WORKING ABROAD

As many banks have offices all over the world, you may have the opportunity to work abroad. In this case language skills will come in useful, so it is a good idea to work hard in your language classes at school.

## Teamworking skills

As well as individual skills, you will also need to be able to work well as part of a team. For most jobs in the finance industry, team working is important, so if you don't work well as part of a group this may not be the career for you. Sometimes, however, you will be expected to work on your own, and at other times you will need to use your initiative to make decisions.

## CASE STUDY

Joshua works as a customer services officer in a retail bank.

*Working in a team is not only good fun, it also makes the job easier. If I ever have a problem there is always someone in my team who can help me.*

## Finding the right job for you

Finding the best career for you involves matching your skills and personality to the skills needed for a particular job. The best way to do this is to start by taking a close look at yourself.

- ◎ Are you good with numbers?
- ◎ Are your communication skills strong?
- ◎ Do you cope well under pressure?
- ◎ Are you always punctual?

There is no point applying to work as an accountant if you can't stand working with numbers and can think of nothing worse than being stuck in an office most of the time.

## CASE STUDY

Sunita is a **human resources** manager in an investment bank.

*Although qualifications are expected when you apply to work here, we place a lot of importance on your personal qualities as well. Are you a team player, for example? How good are you communication skills? We provide very good training, but you have to have the right personal qualities to become successful.*

**below:** *If you have the right skills for the job, you could be a real success in the finance world.*

# SKILLS CHECKLIST

Copy out and fill in the checklist of skills below. Look back at the information in this chapter to see if your skills match up with those required by jobs in the finance industry. Can you identify any area of the industry that you are particularly suited to?

| Skills required | Yes (✔) | No (✔) | Especially important for: |
|---|---|---|---|
| Enjoy working with people | ☐ | ☐ | Retail banking |
| Good analytical skills | ☐ | ☐ | Investment management |
| Good with numbers | ☐ | ☐ | Accountancy |
| Good communication skills | ☐ | ☐ | Retail banking |
| Good IT skills | ☐ | ☐ | All financial jobs |
| Responsible | ☐ | ☐ | Financial advisor |
| Ambitious | ☐ | ☐ | Investment banking |
| Able to remain calm under pressure | ☐ | ☐ | Investment banking |
| Work well in a team | ☐ | ☐ | Retail banking |
| Able to cope with long hours | ☐ | ☐ | Investment banking |
| Language skills | ☐ | ☐ | Working abroad |

# Get ahead!

Draw a table with the following headings:
• IT skills
• customer skills
• team working
• communication skills
Under each heading, write down the things you have done that show you have these skills.

So, do you think you are the right person for a career in finance? If you are ambitious, with excellent communication and analytical skills, you are on the right track.

# Chapter 5

# What qualifications do I need?

Now you know what kind of person would be best suited to working in the finance industry, but what qualifications do you need?

Financial companies are highly selective; they can afford to be, as a lot of high fliers apply to work for them. For this reason they will rarely consider school leavers without qualifications. By gaining a recognized qualification, either through training at work or by taking a full-time course at university, you are likely to have a much wider range of career opportunities and a chance of **promotion**.

There is a whole range of qualifications that can help prepare you for entry to finance jobs, ranging from GCSEs, **National Vocational Qualifications** (NVQs)/**Scottish Vocational Qualifications** (SVQs), A-levels and **internships**, through to degrees and postgraduate qualifications. You need to think about what you want to do within the finance industry – then you can decide which qualifications are most suitable.

### Which qualification?

◎ NVQs/SVQs: These are more practical and less academic than A-levels. They provide a flexible approach to studying a number of different subjects and allow you to progress at your own pace. They have been developed to prepare you for a variety of jobs. You can gain NVQs/SVQs by taking a full-time course at college, or you can study part-time while at work.

◎ **Modern Apprenticeships**: These provide an opportunity to develop skills and expertise and gain NVQs/SVQs while at work.

◎ Further and Higher Education: Many universities and some colleges offer **Higher National Certificate** (HNC), **Higher National Diploma** (HND), or degree courses in Finance and other related subject areas. Examples include HNDs in Business and Finance, and degrees in Accounting and Finance, Economics, or Business Administration.

# Bristol Business School

**above:** *There are many places around the UK where you can study for a qualification in a financial subject.*

◎ Specialist qualifications: Some organizations within the finance industry offer their own qualifications. The Institute of Financial Services (IFS), for example, offers certificates in Personal Finance and Financial Studies.

For the jobs given below, there is no single entry route. The qualifications described are the most common and most relevant for the particular job but are by no means the only qualifications you could consider.

## Retail banks

If you enter a retail bank as a school leaver, for example, working in a clerical position or call centre, you will need five GCSEs, including English and Maths, and two A-levels/Highers. Useful A-level/Higher subjects would include Law, Accountancy, Business Studies, and Economics. Alternatively, you could start on an **apprenticeship** scheme through the Institute of Chartered Financial Services (IFS). Or, you could work towards NVQs/SVQs in Providing Financial Services (Banks and Building Societies).

If you enter a retail bank as a graduate trainee on better pay, you will need a good degree from university, but not necessarily a degree in finance. Relevant subjects include Maths, Business Studies, and Accountancy.

James is training to be a customer advisor in a retail bank.

*I am on an apprenticeship scheme. Most of my training is on the job. I did GCSEs at school and then A-levels in Business Studies and Maths.*

## Accountancy

The minimum entry requirements for accountancy are five GCSEs, including English and Maths, and two A-levels/Highers. Equivalent qualifications such as NVQs/SVQs are also acceptable. However, most people enter accountancy with a university degree, which can be in any subject. You would then work towards **chartered** accountant status through professional exams awarded by the Chartered Institute of Management Accountants (CIMA).

It is also possible for school leavers to follow a **vocational** route through the Institute of Chartered Accountants in England and Wales (ICAEW) or Institute of Chartered Accountants in Scotland (ICAS). This leads to an accounting technician qualification and then on to chartered accountant status.

**left:** *The range of courses available for finance-related qualifications is huge – so make sure you pick one that suits you best!*

There are no formal entry requirements for training as an accounting technician, but employers prefer GCSEs in English and Maths. You will then need to train for an accounting technician qualification while you are at work. This may also lead to NVQs in Accounting.

## Financial advisor

There are no set qualifications required to become a financial advisor. Entrants to this career come from a range of backgrounds and the entry requirements depend on the employer. Most entrants are graduates in business-related subjects. Once in the job, you would work towards professional exams awarded by the Chartered Insurance Institute (CII) or Institute of Financial Services (IFS).

## Insurance broker

There are no formal requirements for the insurance sector. Most employers will require five GCSEs, including English and Maths, and two A-levels/Highers, or equivalent NVQs/SVQs. Many entrants are graduates. Relevant subjects include Insurance, Business Studies, Economics, Law, and Maths, but graduates with Science degrees are also encouraged to apply. It is also possible to enter as a trainee broker technician.

**CASE STUDY**

Gemma is training to be an accounting technician in an accountancy firm.

*I did GCSEs and then an NVQ in Business Management at college. I started work here 6 months ago and am working towards an accounting technician qualification awarded by the Association of Accounting Technicians (AAT). I work part-time, so I have plenty of time to study. I really enjoy the work and can't wait to become qualified. The most important skills you need for my job are a good head for numbers and confidence in using computers.*

Cameron is an insurance broker for a large insurance company.

*I did A-levels in Economics and French, and an NVQ in Sport and Leisure. I then worked in a leisure centre before getting into the insurance industry. I think dealing with customers is the same whichever industry you are in, so my experience with this was excellent training for talking to my insurance customers.*

## Stockbroker, trader, and fund manager

Entrants to a career as a stockbroker, trader, or fund manager are usually graduates. A degree in any subject is acceptable, but Science, Business Studies, Economics, Maths, and Law are particularly relevant. Post-graduate qualifications, such as a Master of Business Administration (MBA), are also useful, as is work experience through an internship.

New entrants to certain jobs in investment management and investment banking must be registered as an "approved person" by the Financial Services Authority (FSA). To gain registration you need to pass an FSA-approved examination such as the Investment Management Certificate.

One thing you should note is that qualifications alone are no guarantee of a job in the finance industry. Much of your success will depend on your personality, attitude, communication skills, and a common sense approach to work and life in general.

**left:** *Whatever qualifications you have, remember that in an interview you will be tested on much more!*

# Chapter 6

# A foot in the door

You are ambitious, have excellent analytical skills, enjoy working with others, and are good with numbers and computers. You seem like the ideal candidate for a position in the finance industry . . . but how do you go about actually getting a job?

## Do well at school

Whatever job you are applying for in the finance industry, most employers look for a good standard of secondary education, including GCSEs (grades A–C) or S-grades (grades 1–3) in English and Maths. This will be a minimum requirement, and while there are opportunities for school leavers to enter retail banks as bank clerks or call centre staff, for most jobs in this industry you will need a university degree. This does not need to be in a finance related subject, but you will need to show evidence of an interest in financial matters.

below: *Numeracy skills are very important for any job in the finance industry.*

## Which subject?

Your Maths and English skills will be important in any job that you do. Most jobs in the finance industry will require you to work with numbers. As a bank clerk, your Maths skills will be useful for dealing with cash, cheques, and card **transactions**.

As an accountant you will be dealing with company accounts, making up long lists of figures, and as a trader or stockbroker you will be dealing with huge sums of money. Mistakes are not an option, so you need to be competent with numbers.

## COMPUTING SKILLS

For most jobs in the finance industry, you will be using a computer. You therefore need to be competent in IT.

Good English skills will be needed for writing formal letters, reports, and sending information round to work colleagues by email. If you have to speak to groups as part of your job, you oral presentation skills also need to be good. Other subjects, such as History and Business Studies, will give you useful communication skills as well.

Foreign languages, such as French, German, Spanish, or Italian, are useful in investment banks with offices all over the world. Ability with a language will open up many more opportunities for you to work abroad.

## The importance of work experience

A relevant qualification will be vital to your employment prospects. However, another key factor that some employers will be looking for is relevant experience, especially experience of working with customers.

**left:** *Keep up your language studies and you could be doing business in Paris, Berlin, or Madrid!*

Relevant work experience can therefore be very important and you should try to gain experience before applying for jobs. You are unlikely to be able to get work experience in a bank, as you need a lot of training to be able to do most jobs. However, there are plenty of things you can do while you are still at school or college that could improve your chances of getting into your chosen career.

### Any job will do!

You may be able to get work experience in the call centre for a bank, but you can also find relevant work experience in many other places. Stacking shelves at a supermarket develops skills in

**above:** *Work experience in any office situation will help develop skills essential for the finance industry.*

stock control and teamwork. Routine office work in any office will develop your ability to deal professionally with colleagues. These are all things employers will look for.

### Internships

Some banks offer internships that you can do during your summer holiday. During this placement you may be **work shadowing** a member of staff. This includes following him or her to see what he or she does in a typical working week, or you may work on an actual project and receive some sort of training. Competition for internships is strong, so you will need to be prepared to work hard to get one. If you are successful, an internship is often a way in, because if you impress those you are working for you are likely to be offered a job with the company.

## The job for you?

Not only is work experience important for impressing employers, it also gives you the chance to find out if this is actually what you want to do as a career. You may have your heart set on working as an accountant, but when you actually start work you may find it is not really for you. Any work experience, whether it is a placement organized by your school or part-time work you have organized yourself, will therefore give you an idea of what the job itself is like and the realities of a working life.

**below:** *Perhaps an office job is not the right one for you after all!*

Once you have completed your work experience, you should think about what you got out of it and make a note of this. Describe any new skills or experiences that you gained such as dealing with customers, working in a team, or making presentations. It will also be very valuable for you to give a presentation about your work experience to your class. This could be as an oral presentation or a written report, or preferably both, so you will build on your communication skills.

## WORK EXPERIENCE

If you have some experience of the world of work under your belt, this will show employers that you are keen and have made an effort to find out about work before applying for a job. It will also make you appear more confident, due to the extra knowledge and skills you will have gained.

## How to stand out from the crowd

Getting a job in the finance industry will be very competitive. There will be lots of enthusiastic, highly qualified young people competing for a limited number of jobs. There may be hundreds of applicants going for the same vacancy. It is therefore not enough to have the relevant qualifications and work experience – you need to stand out from the crowd.

Employers usually look for a broad range of personal skills, including being able to work well in a team, being self-motivated, having good communication skills, and showing an interest in financial affairs. Think about what skills you have to offer and spend some time finding out about the financial markets. You can do this by reading publications such as the *Financial Times* and the *Economist*.

**below:** *Financial publications are a good place to start looking for jobs and finding out about the qualifications required for the role.*

## Applying for jobs

To find out what jobs are on offer in the finance industry, you can search in a number of places.

◎ Look in newspapers, both local and national, for job adverts.

◎ Talk to your careers advisor at school.

◎ Visit the careers section of your local library.

◎ Look for the names of companies that you might be interested in working for on the Internet and in brochures. You can then write to them to see if they have any suitable work.

◎ Search the Internet for jobs. Use the website www.totaljobs.com, for example.

◎ Visit job centres and recruitment agencies.

Some examples of the types of job vacancies you might see in your local paper are shown below:

### FINANCIAL ANALYST

**Salary: £23,000 to £27,000 per year**

A large investment management company seeks a graduate (preferably with an Economics, Banking or Finance degree) for the role of financial analyst. Candidates must have strong numeracy, financial, and computing skills. IT skills are also essential.

### CHIEF ACCOUNTANT

Salary: £70,000 + car + pension

An IT business has an excellent opening in its head office for a chief accountant. You will oversee an accounts team of five people and will take responsibility for monthly and year-end reporting. You will have extensive technical accounting experience and will be comfortable with large computerised accounting systems. Ideal for an experienced chartered accountant looking for a long-term opportunity.

### Finance Graduate

**Salary: £18,000 to £22,000**

A leading employer within the investment banking environment is looking to recruit two finance graduates who possess the drive and desire to succeed in the world of investment banking. The ideal candidate will possess a finance or business related degree, be very self-motivated, and have excellent IT and communication skills.

When you apply for a job, you will either have to fill in an application form or provide a curriculum vitae (CV). Whichever method you use, this will be the first impression the employer gets of you, so you need to get it right.

**right:** *Make sure anything you send to a prospective employer is neat and legible.*

## Completing application forms

If the employer sends you an application form, then you must use this to apply for the job. The first thing you should do is photocopy the form, so you can create a rough draft on the photocopy. This way, if you make any mistakes, it does not matter.

Read through all the questions before you start, and then take your time to fill in the answers. Make sure you answer the questions actually asked and always be honest in your answers. If you make things up, the chances are you will be found out if you reach the interview stage.

Before you fill your form in, it is very useful to try and work out what the employer will be looking for. Write down everything you think they will want to see evidence of on your application form. Then write down the skills you have that would be relevant to those required by the employer. They might be things you have done in school projects, your work experience, or one of your hobbies.

Once you have checked your form for spelling mistakes, grammar, and punctuation, you can copy it on to the original application form. Keep your writing neat and tidy and check the form again before sending it off – or better still, get someone else to check it for you. Make sure you post it well before the closing date and use a suitable envelope. Do not fold your application form. Keep the photocopy in case you get an interview and need to check what you wrote.

Follow all the instructions on the form.

Make sure you begin with your most recent job or placement.

Include any part-time work you have done.

Describe any relevant hobbies you may have.

State why you are interested in the job.

Include any relevant skills and experience that you have not already mentioned.

**APPLICATION FORM**
Please use black ink

**Job title**

**PERSONAL DETAILS**
First name          Surname
Address             Date of birth
                    Phone number
Post code           E-mail address

**WORK EXPERIENCE**
Begin with your most recent employment. Include any work experience or voluntary work.

| Employer's name | Your title | Dates of employment |
| | | From          To |
| | | |
| | | |
| | | |

**QUALIFICATIONS**
Begin with your most recent qualifications.

| Subject/Course | Level (Standard, Higher, SVQ, Unit, Other) | Year taken | Final result |
| | | | |
| | | | |
| | | | |
| | | | |

**PERSONAL PROFILE**
Use this space to give any additional information that may be of interest to the employer.

**REFERENCE**
Please provide the name and address of someone who can be asked for a reference.

| Name and job title | Address | Telephone number |
| | | |
| | | |

I confirm that the information on this form is true and correct to the best of my knowledge.

Signature                    Date

## CVs and covering letters

A CV is a form that tells employers about your education, experience, and interests. Some employers will ask for a CV instead of sending you an application form to fill in. When you write your CV you will need to include all the information that the employer would have requested from you on an application form. You will also need to send a covering letter explaining why you are applying for the job.

An example of a CV is shown below. As you can see, it has been typed and has a clear layout.

It first gives your personal details, such as your name, address, and school. It then describes your qualifications, work experience, and interests.

Do not try to include too much information on your CV as this will make it difficult to read. It should not be more than two pages long.

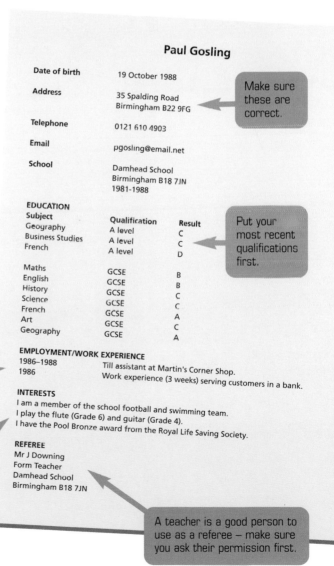

**Paul Gosling**

| | |
|---|---|
| Date of birth | 19 October 1988 |
| Address | 35 Spalding Road<br>Birmingham B22 9FG |
| Telephone | 0121 610 4903 |
| Email | pgosling@email.net |
| School | Damhead School<br>Birmingham B18 7JN<br>1981-1988 |

Make sure these are correct.

**EDUCATION**

| Subject | Qualification | Result |
|---|---|---|
| Geography | A level | C |
| Business Studies | A level | C |
| French | A level | D |
| Maths | GCSE | B |
| English | GCSE | B |
| History | GCSE | C |
| Science | GCSE | C |
| French | GCSE | A |
| Art | GCSE | C |
| Geography | GCSE | A |

Put your most recent qualifications first.

**EMPLOYMENT/WORK EXPERIENCE**

| | |
|---|---|
| 1986–1988 | Till assistant at Martin's Corner Shop. |
| 1986 | Work experience (3 weeks) serving customers in a bank. |

**INTERESTS**
I am a member of the school football and swimming team.
I play the flute (Grade 6) and guitar (Grade 4).
I have the Pool Bronze award from the Royal Life Saving Society.

**REFEREE**
Mr J Downing
Form Teacher
Damhead School
Birmingham B18 7JN

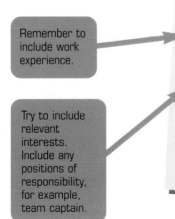

Remember to include work experience.

Try to include relevant interests. Include any positions of responsibility, for example, team captain.

A teacher is a good person to use as a referee – make sure you ask their permission first.

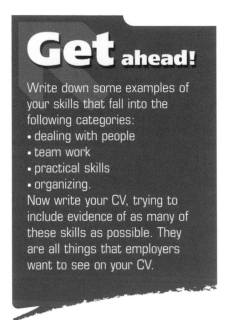

# Get ahead!

Write down some examples of your skills that fall into the following categories:
• dealing with people
• team work
• practical skills
• organizing.

Now write your CV, trying to include evidence of as many of these skills as possible. They are all things that employers want to see on your CV.

You will need to stress all your good points on your CV, but you must be honest. If you play netball for your school team do not be tempted to exaggerate and say you play netball for England. If you get an interview, you will be asked lots of questions about what is on your CV, so if you exaggerated anything, you will soon be found out. Once you have created your CV you will need to check it very carefully for spelling mistakes, grammar, and punctuation.

You should always send a handwritten or typed covering letter with your CV (see left). This letter should explain why you are sending your CV and why you are applying for the job. You need to make your covering letter specific to the job you are applying for. Always address it to a specific person – never write "Dear Sir/Madam". You may need to contact the organization by telephone to find out who to address it to. In your letter you should show that you know something about the company.

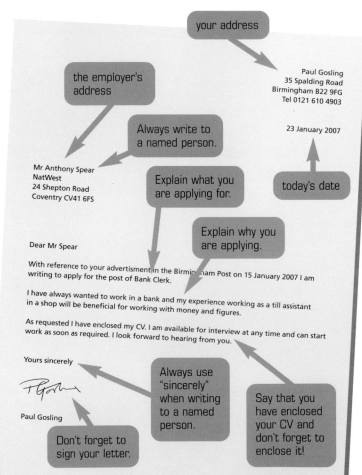

your address

the employer's address

Always write to a named person.

Explain what you are applying for.

today's date

Explain why you are applying.

Paul Gosling
35 Spalding Road
Birmingham B22 9FG
Tel 0121 610 4903

23 January 2007

Mr Anthony Spear
NatWest
24 Shepton Road
Coventry CV41 6FS

Dear Mr Spear

With reference to your advertisement in the Birmingham Post on 15 January 2007 I am writing to apply for the post of Bank Clerk.

I have always wanted to work in a bank and my experience working as a till assistant in a shop will be beneficial for working with money and figures.

As requested I have enclosed my CV. I am available for interview at any time and can start work as soon as required. I look forward to hearing from you.

Yours sincerely

Paul Gosling

Always use "sincerely" when writing to a named person.

Say that you have enclosed your CV and don't forget to enclose it!

Don't forget to sign your letter.

## Interviews

Congratulations! You have sent off you CV or application form and have been invited to an interview. Do not celebrate too soon though – there are probably many other people who have also got this far. Employers interview a lot of people to try and find the best person for the job. You therefore have to show the interviewer that you are that person.

There are a number of things you can do to prepare yourself for an interview. The first thing you should do is find out everything you can about the company and what the job involves. You can even prepare some questions to ask the interviewer about the job. After all, the interview is also an opportunity for you to find out if you would like to work in that particular job. You should read through your application form or CV to remind yourself of how you answered any questions.

## ASSESSMENT CENTRES

If you get through the first round of interviews for a graduate finance job you may be invited to an assessment centre. This will most likely take the form of a 2-day event, where you must participate in activities designed to test your ability to solve problems, present ideas, and work with other people. You will be being assessed the whole time you are there, even over dinner.

**below:** *First impressions count! Make sure you are smartly dressed and in plenty of time for your interview.*

In the interview itself the most important thing to do is relax and be yourself. Be enthusiastic and answer all the questions clearly. If you do not understand a question ask the interviewer to explain it, and don't worry if you do not know the answer to every question you are asked. Just be honest and do not make things up – a good interviewer will know when you are doing this. Remember to be positive and sell yourself.

## SOME COMMON INTERVIEW QUESTIONS

Think of answers to these questions before you go for an interview. They are the type of questions interviewers like to ask.

◎ **Why do you want this job?**
◎ **Why do you think you would be good at this job?**
◎ **What are your strengths?**
◎ **What are your weaknesses?**
◎ **What did you like about your work experience?**
◎ **What did you learn from your work experience?**
◎ **What do you think are the important qualities for this job?**
◎ **What do you know about this company?**
◎ **How would your friends or family describe you?**
◎ **How do you work well in a team and can you give any examples?**
◎ **How do you stay organized?**
◎ **What do you think would be the worst part of this job?**

When the interview is over, it is unlikely that you will find out if you got the job straight away. The company will usually have lots more people to interview before a decision is made. When you do get the result, do not give up if you are unsuccessful – after all, you may have come a close second. Ask the interviewer for feedback. This way you should be able to work out why you didn't get the job and will be able to do better next time.

# Chapter 7

# Onwards and upwards

Imagine that you have done well at school, obtained all the relevant qualifications, skills, and experience, applied for your ideal job in the finance industry, and been successful. Congratulations! So what happens now? How do you shape your career? What opportunities are there for further training and advancement up the career ladder?

## On-the-job training

Most employers will provide some form of on-the-job training when you start working for them. Once you are settled in your job there may be further opportunities to train at work and you should take advantage of these. In order to do well in your chosen career, and hopefully to move onwards and upwards, it is a good idea to get as much training as possible.

*below: You will be able to take advantage of ongoing training while you are at work.*

Banks offer excellent training at all levels. In a retail bank you will receive a combination of:

◎ in-house training – training offered by people in the same company
◎ residential courses – for example, where you go on a course for a week in a hotel
◎ distance learning – via the Internet, usually in your own time.

All staff can expect to attend regular training courses throughout their career, to keep up to date with new developments.

Graduate trainees will take part in a structured training programme for up to 2 years from when they start working. This training will be a combination of classroom teaching, on-the-job work experience, computer-based training, and working alongside more senior staff.

**right:** *As a financial analyst you never stop learning.*

## CASE STUDY

James is a graduate trainee in an investment bank.

*I have received a mixture of training since I started working here. I was in the classroom for the first 3 months. I then did some work experience in three different departments, to give me a feel for the whole organization. During this time I was given specific projects to work on, so I was made to feel like part of the team, although it meant a lot of responsibility as well.*

Nearly 75 per cent of all financial companies in the UK have employees working towards professional qualifications. Accountants and financial advisors, for example, work towards professional exams to qualify for chartered status, awarded by the Chartered Institute of Management Accountants (CIMA), Chartered Insurance Institute (CII), or Institute of Financial Services (IFS). This will include some **distance learning**, as well as on-the-job training.

Once chartered status has been achieved the training still continues. In most financial institutions training will be an ongoing feature of your job, and you will be expected to keep up to date with changes and trends in your part of the industry.

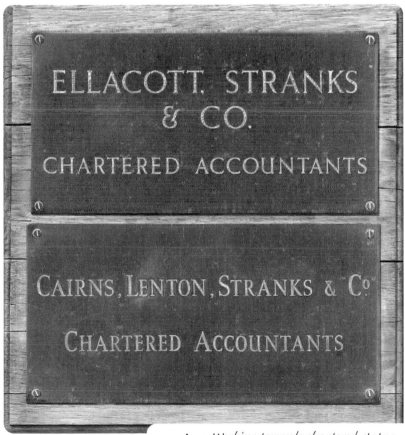

**above:** *Working towards chartered status requires a lot of hard work and dedication, but it can certainly help your career.*

# Where do I go next?

Your prospects for promotion depend on your ability and performance in your job. Many jobs offer the opportunity for promotion to supervisory or managerial levels, but promotion is difficult. The advances in technology mean that more people are now applying for fewer jobs.

It used to be usual that young people entering a bank or insurance company worked their way up from the bottom and probably stayed with that organization all their working lives. Today, if you begin your career as a bank clerk and wish to move up into management you will need to study for professional qualifications, for example, the Professional Diploma in Financial Services Management offered by the Institute of Financial Services (IFS). You may also need to move from branch to branch, maybe to a different city, or even abroad, in order to move up the career ladder. It will all depend on where the opportunities arise. However, if you are prepared to work hard and keep moving, you should be able to advance in your career.

## CASE STUDY

Marcus works as an investment analyst for an investment management company.

*As soon as I started work I was given a huge pile of books and had to start studying for my Chartered Financial Analyst (CFA) qualification. This is an excellent qualification to have, but is incredibly hard work. I have been on 3-week long courses as part of the training, but I have to do most of the studying in my own time. It takes 3 years and I have just 1 more year to go. It will certainly be a relief when it is all over.*

Once you are fully qualified as an accountant or financial advisor, you could move into a senior management position and earn a lot of money, or you could choose to become self-employed, offering consultancy services to clients. New career paths may also open up after you qualify and you may be able to move into specialist areas of your profession. An accountant, for example, may move into industry and commerce accountancy.

## TRANSFERABLE SKILLS

People who succeed in the finance industry develop a range of communication and people skills that can also be useful in other jobs. Within the industry there are plenty of opportunities at all levels for you to create an interesting career for yourself. However, for some there may come a time when you feel the need to move out of the industry, and these so-called **transferable skills** will enable you to do that.

For those who enter investment banking with the right skills and abilities, there is the potential to rise quickly to positions carrying a lot of responsibility. People in these positions are well rewarded.

**below:** *You could progress to become a manager, either within the finance industry or in a new area of work.*

Are you still interested in pursuing a career in finance? The industry can certainly offer you a challenging and varied career, with plenty of opportunities for promotion and for making money. You will have to work hard to get there though, as a lot of people see finance as a rewarding industry to work in. Many people also think that working in this area will make them instantly rich. You know better than that! You know that the hours you work are likely to be long, and that you will not be given huge bonuses at the beginning of your career.

## Making the right choice

You need to think very carefully about what you want from your career. Different people want different things, and the sooner you decide what you want to do, the sooner you can start working towards gaining the relevant qualifications.

You also need to decide if you are the right person to enjoy working in the finance industry. It is certainly not for everyone. As competition for jobs is likely to be strong you need to have the right personality and the right skills, as well as the right qualifications. As if this is not enough already, you will need to show some evidence that you are interested in a career in finance, either through relevant work experience, an internship, or by reading the relevant newspapers and publications. Once you have thought carefully about all of this you will be well placed for applying for a job in the finance industry. Then all you need to do is stand out from the crowd. Good luck!

**LEARNING PLAN**

Map out a 5-year learning plan to expand your talents and get a head start. For example:
- Year 1: I would like to get five GCSEs grade C or above
- Year 2: I would like to study Business Studies at A-level

And so on...

Monique successfully completed her Chartered Institute of Insurance exams in 2004.

*I chose to do a degree in Business and Finance at the University of Sheffield, and have never looked back! I managed to get on to a 2-year graduate trainee scheme with one of the biggest insurance companies in the country. I chose this route as I wanted to move around within the company and try different areas of work before committing to one in particular. I am so glad I did this, as I feel I got a really good overview of the business.*

*Three years down the line I have been promoted to claims supervisor, manage two different teams, and have completed my CII exams. I think my time on the graduate trainee scheme helped me to choose the direction I wanted to take within insurance, and gave me the confidence to move quickly towards promotion. I would advise anyone interested in a career in finance to think about a graduate scheme as a way in – it can definitely give you a head start!*

**below:** *The right qualification can be a good start in the finance industry.*

## Jobs in finance

- ◎ Accountant
- ◎ Accounting technician
- ◎ Accounts clerk
- ◎ Actuary
- ◎ Auditor
- ◎ Bank cashier
- ◎ Bank clerk
- ◎ Bank manager
- ◎ Branch manager
- ◎ Business development manager
- ◎ Credit analyst
- ◎ Credit manager
- ◎ Customer services manager
- ◎ Financial advisor
- ◎ Financial analyst
- ◎ Financial counsellor
- ◎ Fund manager
- ◎ Insurance broker
- ◎ Insurance claims settler
- ◎ Insurance underwriter
- ◎ Lending clerk
- ◎ Pensions advisor
- ◎ Risk analyst
- ◎ Stockbroker
- ◎ Trader

# Careers websites

*Please note that qualifications and courses are subject to change.*

- City and Guilds (www.city-and-guilds.co.uk)
  - This website tells you all about City and Guilds qualifications.
- Connexions Direct (www.connexions-direct.com)
  - This website gives advice to young people, including learning and careers. Includes link to the Jobs4U careers database.
- Learndirect (www.learndirect-advice.co.uk) and Learndirect Scotland (www.learndirectscotland.com/)
  - Go to "job profiles" for details of many jobs in finance and courses and qualifications.
- Modern Apprenticeships, Scotland (www.scottish-enterprise.com/modernapprenticeships)
  - Check out the case studies of people already training.
- Need2Know: Learning (www.need2know.co.uk/learning)
  - This site gives information about studying and qualifications.
- Qualifications and Curriculum Authority (www.qca.org.uk/14-19)
  - Go to "Qualifications" and click on "Main qualification groups" to find out about NVQs.
- Scottish Vocational Qualifications (www.sqa.org.uk)
  - You can find out all the latest qualifications information here.
- The National Council for Work Experience (www.work-experience.org)
  - Go to "Students and Graduates" to search for placements.

# Get ahead in finance!

- Association of Accounting Technicians (AAT) – www.aat.org.uk
- Association of Independent Financial Advisers (AIFA)
  - www.aifa.net
- Charted Institute of Management Accountants (CIMA)
  - www.cimaglobal.com
- Financial job marketplace – www.efinancialcareers.co.uk
- Institute of Financial Services/Chartered Institute of Banking
  - www.ifslearning.com

**acquisition** when one company buys another company

**apprenticeship** training scheme that allows you to work for money, learn, and become qualified at the same time

**bank account** arrangement you have with a bank where they look after your money

**bank clerk** person who deals with customers in a high street bank

**benefit** extra perk that you may be given when you work for a company, for example, free private healthcare

**brokerage** arranging deals

**call centre** part of a bank or other business where staff respond to customer phone calls

**chartered** when someone has completed special exams to become qualified

**cheque** printed sheet of paper from a bank that you can use instead of money

**commercial** related to business

**commission** amount of money paid to someone for a service

**compensation** money given to you if you have insurance and are injured

**credit card** small plastic card used to buy things

**currency** type of money that a country uses

**distance learning** method of studying where lessons are broadcast on television or over the Internet

**expenditure** amount of money that goes out of a business, for example, what they spend

**financial year** period of a year over which the accounts are calculated, usually from 1 April to 31 March

**foreign exchange** place where you can buy and sell foreign money

**Higher National Certificate** (HNC) technical qualification that you can take after a National Certificate or after A-levels/ Highers

**Higher National Diploma** (HND) technical qualification that you progress to from an HNC (see HNC). Usually takes 2 years to achieve.

**human resources** department in business that recruits and looks after the interests of all members of staff

**income** amount of money that comes in to a business

**initiative** ability to make your own decisions

**internship** position offered by a company to provide training and work experience, usually to a student in their final year of study

**invest** buy shares in a company in order to make a profit, as these shares increase in value over time

**merger** when two or more companies join together to form one large company

**Modern Apprenticeship** Scottish apprenticeship, lasts for 4 years

**mortgage** when you borrow money from a bank in order to buy a house

**multitasking** doing lots of different things at the same time

**National Vocational Qualification** (NVQ) in England and Wales, a work-related, competence-based qualification that shows you have the knowledge and skills to do a job effectively. NVQs represent national standards that are recognized by employers throughout the UK.

**overdraft** amount of money you owe a bank when you take out more money than you have in your account

**pension** regular payment made to someone who is retired

**promotion** move to a more important job in a company

**regulate** control activities to make sure everyone plays by the rules

**salary** money that you receive as payment from your employer

**Scottish Vocational Qualification** (SVQ) in Scotland, a work-related, competence based qualification that shows you have the knowledge and skills to do a job effectively. SVQs represent national standards that are recognized by employers throughout the UK.

**service industry** business that does work for a customer such as banking or retail

**share** part of a company, so when you buy a share you own part of that company

**stock** money made by a company for the issue of shares (see shares)

**stock market** business of buying and selling stocks and shares

**student loan** method of paying for your education where you borrow money from the government and pay it back when you start working

**subsidized** when part of the cost of something is already paid for, so you pay less for it

**take-over** gain control of a company by buying most of its shares

**time zone** one of the 24 areas that the world is divided into, each of which has its own time

**transferable skills** skills that you have learnt at school or in a job that can be used in another job

**transaction** action you take in a bank such as paying money into your account

**underwrite** support a business financially

**university fees** amount of money you have to pay in order to go to university

**vocational** related to the world of work and careers

**work shadowing** following a more senior employee at work to find out what their job involves

# Titles in the *How to get ahead in* series include:

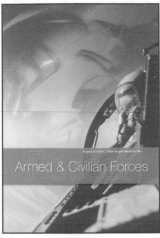

Hardback 978 1 4062 0450 6

Hardback 978 1 4062 0448 3

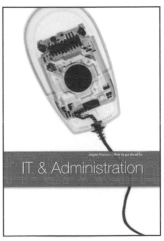

Hardback 978 1 4062 0449 0

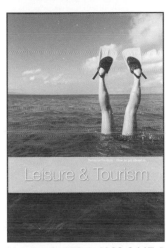

Hardback 978 1 4062 0447 6

Hardback 978 1 4062 0446 9

Other titles available:

| | |
|---|---|
| Beauty | Hardback 978 1 4062 0442 1 |
| Catering | Hardback 978 1 4062 0443 8 |
| Construction | Hardback 978 1 4062 0440 7 |
| Engineering and Design | Hardback 978 1 4062 0441 4 |
| Healthcare | Hardback 978 1 4062 0444 5 |

Find out about the other titles in this series on our website at www.raintreepublishers.co.uk